Worldoflogan.com

LOGAN
AND THE JUNGLE MOUNTAIN

Bruce Goddard

illustrated by Zina Jugai

Logan always loved an adventure.

His favourite place in the big jungle was in his very own
imagination. When he closed his eyes and dreamed big
dreams, he could go anywhere and achieve anything.

One day, Logan woke up from a daydream and wanted to visit the top of the jungle mountain, but he did not know how to do it as no lion had ever done it before. He just knew that he wanted to.

"Daddy, do you think I can get to the top of the mountain? No lion has ever been there before, and I don't know how," Logan asked daddy lion.

"Yes, of course you can. Remember, you do not always need to know how, you just need to know exactly what you want and **imagine** what it would **feel** like if you were already there. Nature always guides us about which way to go."

Logan began his adventure and walked towards the jungle mountain far, far away.

As he was walking, he imagined that he was already at the top of the jungle mountain with its beautiful views, a welcoming cave and some of the tastiest food he'd ever had.

As Logan walked towards a stream, he came across a tiger.
"Where are you going to, little lion?" asked the tiger whilst
drinking from the stream.
"I am going to the top of the jungle mountain," replied
Logan.

"You can't go there, no jungle cat has ever been so high," the tiger laughed.
"Well, I am going to be the first," Logan said.
"Well, best of luck," chuckled the tiger and went on his way.

After seeing the tiger, Logan doubted whether he could get to the top of the jungle mountain, but then he remembered what daddy lion said about imagination.

Logan found the shade of a tree, closed his eyes and sang,

"I am happy, so so so happy! I am now at the top of the mountain, and I'm having so much fun, fun, fun. I feel as high as a bird, and no other animals can be heard."

Logan got up once he imagined and had the feeling of being at the top of the mountain.

Logan continued his adventure and came across a group of friendly monkeys.

"Where are you going to, little lion?" asked one of the monkeys swinging from a tree.
"I am going to the top of the jungle mountain," replied Logan.

"You can't go there, only birds have ever been so high," said the monkey, bursting with laughter.
"Well, I am going to be the first lion," Logan said.
"Well, best of luck," the monkeys chuckled and went on their way.

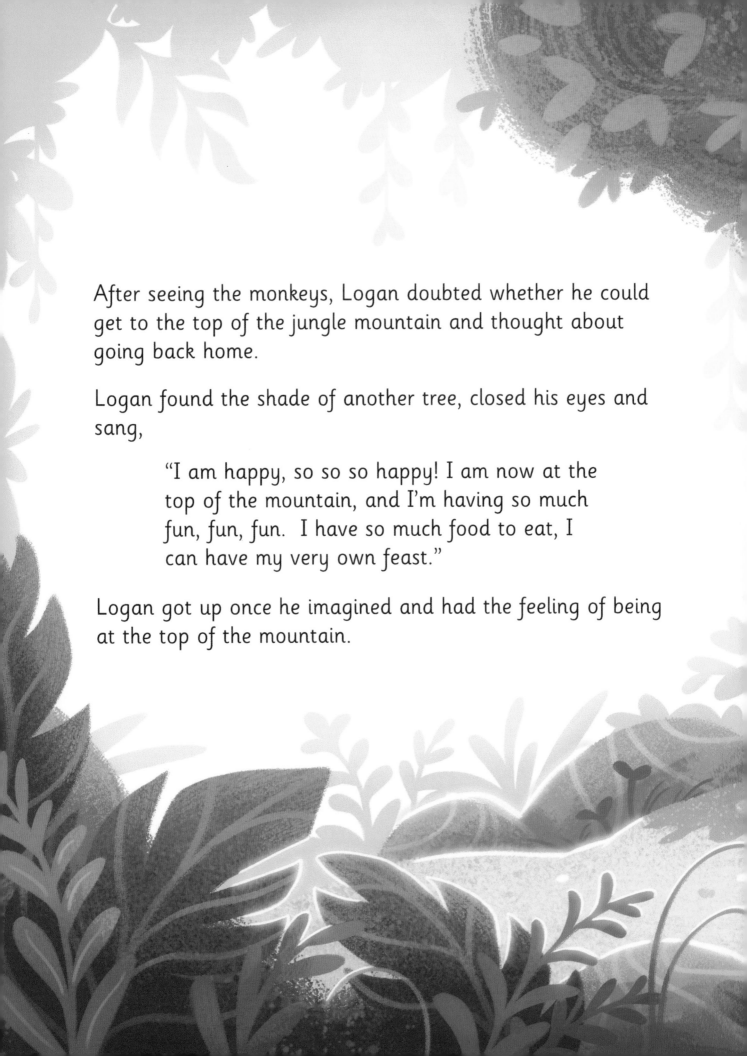

After seeing the monkeys, Logan doubted whether he could get to the top of the jungle mountain and thought about going back home.

Logan found the shade of another tree, closed his eyes and sang,

"I am happy, so so so happy! I am now at the top of the mountain, and I'm having so much fun, fun, fun. I have so much food to eat, I can have my very own feast."

Logan got up once he imagined and had the feeling of being at the top of the mountain.

Logan continued his adventure and came across a big bear.

"Where are you going to, little lion?" asked a bear whilst scratching his back on a large pear tree.
This time, Logan stopped, thought, and replied with a big smile, "I'd love to talk, but I am going for a very long walk."
"That's okay, enjoy your walk, and we can talk when you come back this way," said the bear with a smile.

"That sounds great, have a great day,"
replied Logan and went on his way.

This time, Logan didn't feel the need to find the shade of a large tree as he continued to imagine and sing.

After a very long journey, he came to the bottom of the jungle mountain. He walked up higher and higher, and it became harder and harder, and Logan became increasingly tired.

Just as he was about to rest,
Logan peeked over.

Logan finally reached the top of the jungle mountain and shouted, 'I DID IT! I DID IT!' His big dream was challenging, but with focus and dedication, it was all worth it, as the top of the jungle mountain had amazing jungle views, enough food for a feast and a cave for a well-deserved rest.

Worldoflogan.com

Follow Logan
Fun Activities & Adventures

@WorldofLoganOfficial